Numeracy Focus

Class Focus Book 3

Mike Askew • Sheila Ebbutt

RIGBY

1	2	3	4	5	6	7	8	9	10
11	12	13	14	15	16	17	18	19	20
21	22	23	24	25	26	27	28	29	30
31	32	33	34	35	36	37	38	39	40
41	42	43	44	45	46	47	48	49	50
51	52	53	54	55	56	57	58	59	60
61	62	63	64	65	66	67	68	69	70
71	72	73	74	75	76	77	78	79	80
81	82	83	84	85	86	87	88	89	90
91	92	93	94	95	96	97	98	99	100

Place value grid

100	200	300	400	500	600	700	800	900
10	20	30	40	50	60	70	80	90
1	2	3	4	5	6	7	8	9

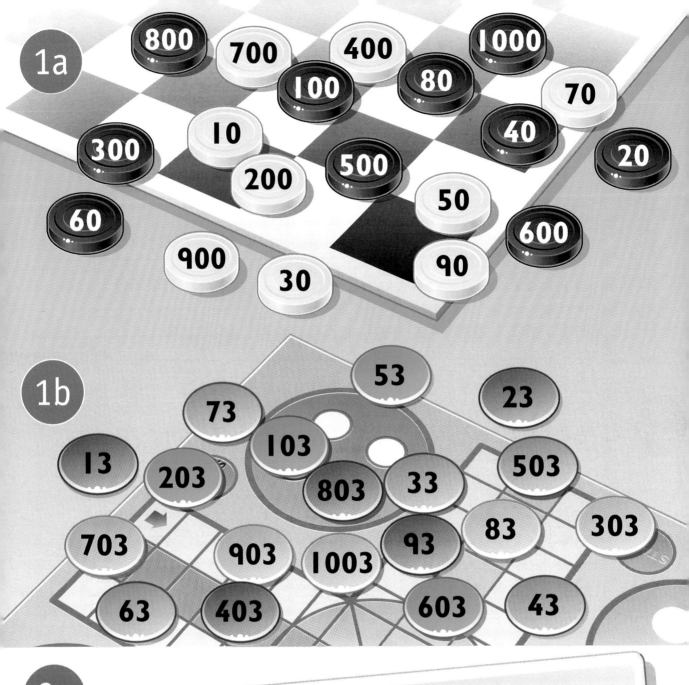

1a

800, 700, 400, 1000, 100, 80, 70, 10, 300, 40, 20, 200, 500, 50, 60, 600, 900, 90, 30

1b

53, 73, 23, 103, 13, 203, 503, 803, 33, 703, 83, 303, 903, 1003, 93, 63, 403, 603, 43

2a

Addition and subtraction words

- and
- take away
- add
- less
- increase
- take away from

- sum
- subtract
- total
- decrease
- together
- difference

- difference between
- count on
- count back
- altogether
- make
- makes

- equal
- minus
- equals
- leaves
- plus
- more

A

① 8 + 11 = ☐   11 + 8 = ☐

② 2 + 14 = ☐   14 + 2 = ☐

③ 18 + 1 = ☐   1 + 18 = ☐

④ 16 + 3 = ☐   3 + 16 = ☐

B

① 2 + 13 + 8 = ☐   ② 7 + 5 + 13 = ☐

③ 15 + 2 + 5 = ☐   ④ 4 + 11 + 6 = ☐

⑤ 13 + 5 + 7 = ☐   ⑥ 11 + 4 + 9 = ☐

3a

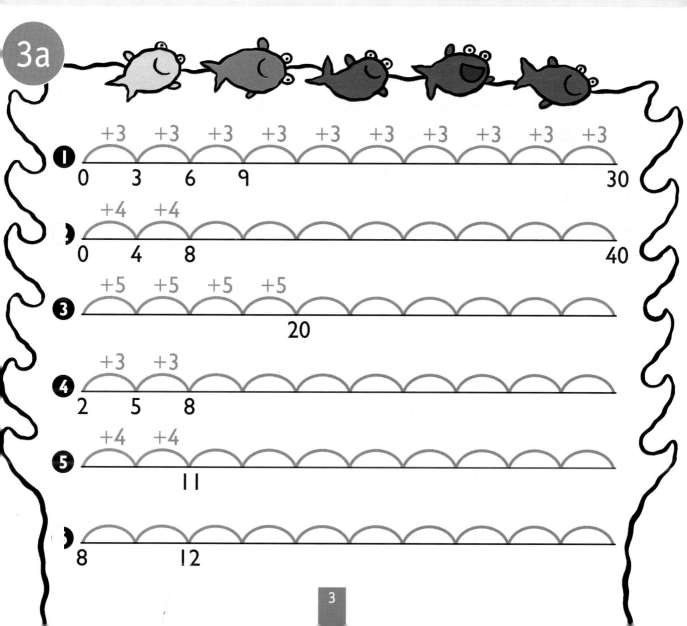

① +3 +3 +3 +3 +3 +3 +3 +3 +3 +3
0 3 6 9   30

② +4 +4
0 4 8   40

③ +5 +5 +5 +5
          20

④ +3 +3
2 5 8

⑤ +4 +4
      11

⑥
8   12

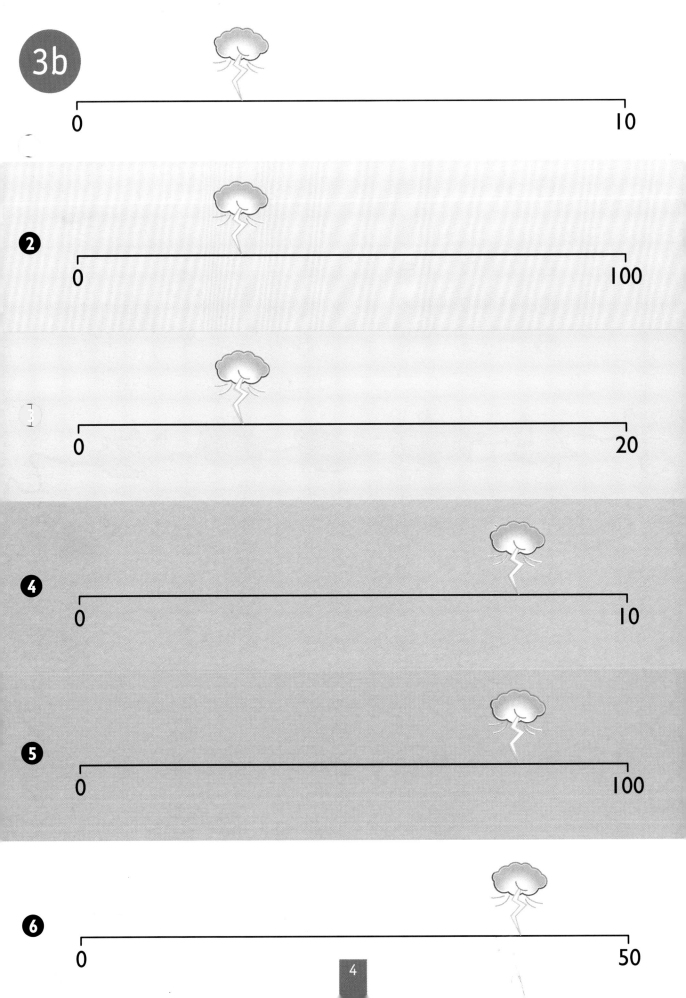

3b

0   10

2

0   100

0   20

4

0   10

5

0   100

6

0   50

Make a skeleton of a cube.
You need:
12 straws and 8 lumps
of Blu-tack.

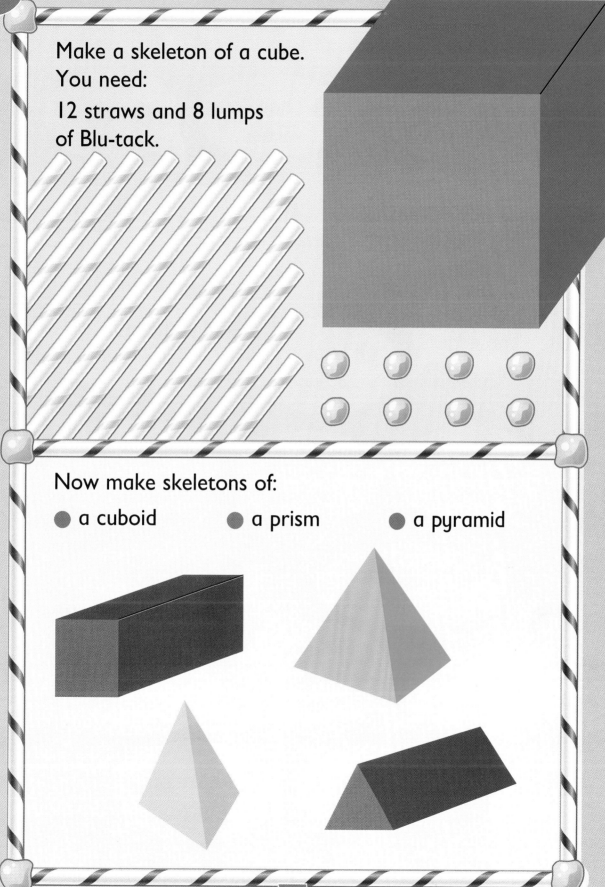

Now make skeletons of:

● a cuboid   ● a prism   ● a pyramid

1 I have one circular face.

2 I have one vertex.

3 I slide.

4 All my faces are square.

5 All my faces are triangles.

6 I have no edges.

7 I have 8 edges.

8 I have 2 circular faces.

9 I have no vertices.

10 I have 8 vertices.

11 I have a square base.

12 2 of my faces are triangles.

13 3 of my faces are rectangles.

14 I have 6 vertices.

15 I have 4 triangular faces.

16 I roll smoothly.

17 My base is a circle.

18 I have only 4 faces.

1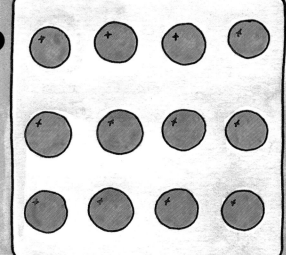

2

3

4

5

6

1 Harry cooks small cakes in baking trays.
In each tray there are 5 equal rows and 3 cakes in each row.
How many cakes are there in each tray?

2 Harry puts out 20 cakes to cool. He lays them out in rows of 4.
How many rows of cakes does he put out?

3 Harry packs biscuits in packets of 6.
How many biscuits does he need to fill 4 packets?

4 The doughnut machine puts doughnuts out in rows of 4.
There are 5 rows of doughnuts.
How many doughnuts are there altogether?

5 Harry puts 18 doughnuts into boxes. Each box holds 3 doughnuts.
How many boxes does Harry fill?

6 Harry puts 12 cherry buns and 13 raspberry buns in a bag.
How many buns are there altogether in the bag?

7a

A You have 3 hoops.

What total scores can you make?

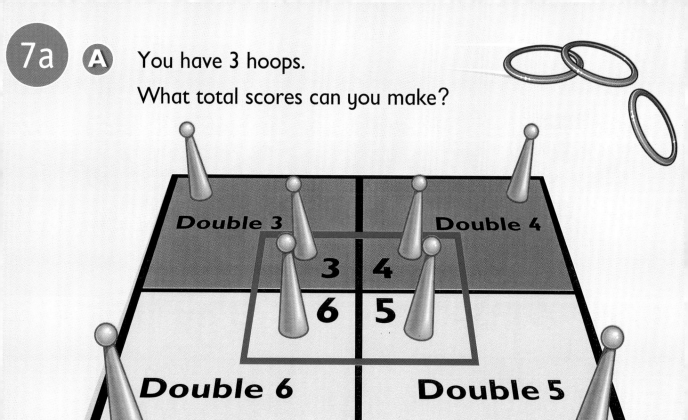

Double 3 · Double 4

| 3 | 4 |
| 6 | 5 |

Double 6 · Double 5

B You have 3 hoops.

What total scores can you make?

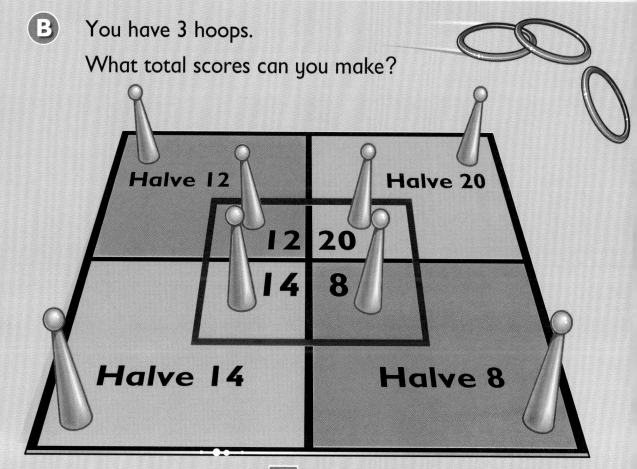

Halve 12 · Halve 20

| 12 | 20 |
| 14 | 8 |

Halve 14 · Halve 8

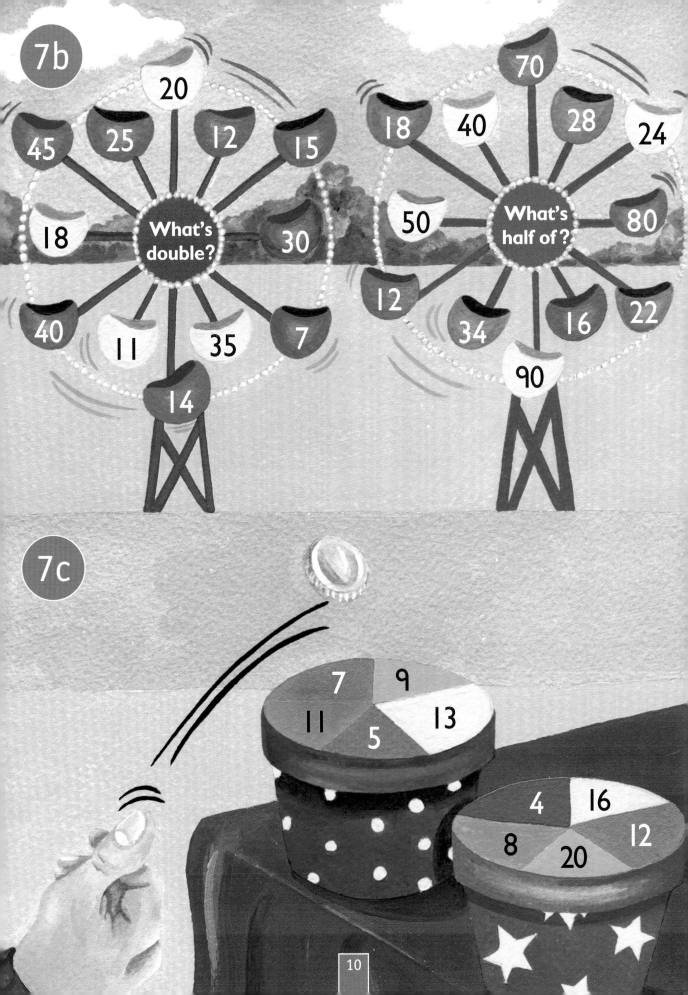

8 **A** Add 9.

56　23　77　45　91　21

90　93　47　50　11　28

5　30　49　26　18　7

86　85　61　42　84　44

B Add 11.

74　10　48　60　89

79　68　6　92　18

9　73　50　87　33

64　23　78　1　22

34　25　31　2　7

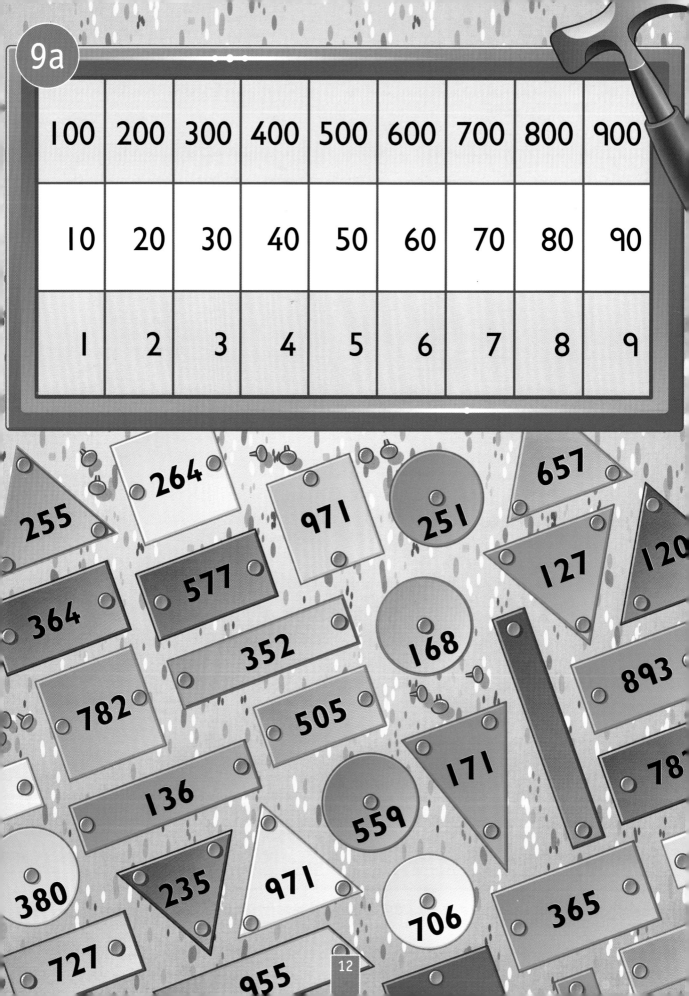

Three hundred and fifty-six

356

300 + 50 + 6

1. Eight hundred and thirty-three

2. 700 + 50 + 1

3. 979

4. 200 + 30 + 7

5. 900 + 10 + 6

6. 136

7. Three hundred and ninety-seven

8. 370

9. 100 + 10

10. 691

11. Four hundred and twenty-four

12. 783

13. 500 + 30 + 6

14. Six hundred and one

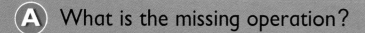

A What is the missing operation?

1 375 ? 385

2 741 ? 641

3 499 ? 599

4 516 ? 515

5 498 ? 488

6 734 ? 834

7 273 ? 283

8 857 ? 847

9 242 ? 243

10 221 ? 121

B Copy and complete.

1 264 ? 364

2 245 ? 145

3 587 ? 597

4 518 ? 418

5 372 ? 371

6 631 ? 731

7 541 ? 542

8 182 ? 282

9 756 ? 856

10 274 ? 174

10a

❶ 24 people travelled to a party. 4 people went in each car. How many cars did they use?

❷ They had 24 cans of fizzy drink. There are 4 cans to a box. How many boxes were there?

❸ 24 people played party games in equal teams. There were 6 teams. How many people to each team?

❹ There were 6 sweets in each party bag. 4 children were each given a party bag. They put all their sweets into a bowl. How many sweets were there altogether?

10b

❶ Anne has 19 stickers to give away. 3 friends share her stickers equally. How many stickers does each friend get?

❷ Jim has 2 pen cases. He has 22 pens. Each case holds 10 pens. Can he fit all his pens in the cases?

❸ Pencils cost 20p. Raj has 90p. How many pencils can Raj buy? Does he have any money left?

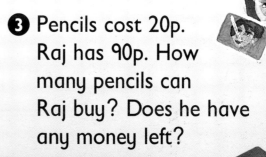

❹ Erasers cost 5p. Mona has 37p. How many erasers can she buy? How much money does she have left?

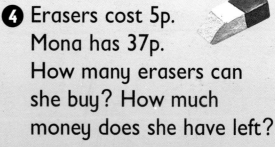

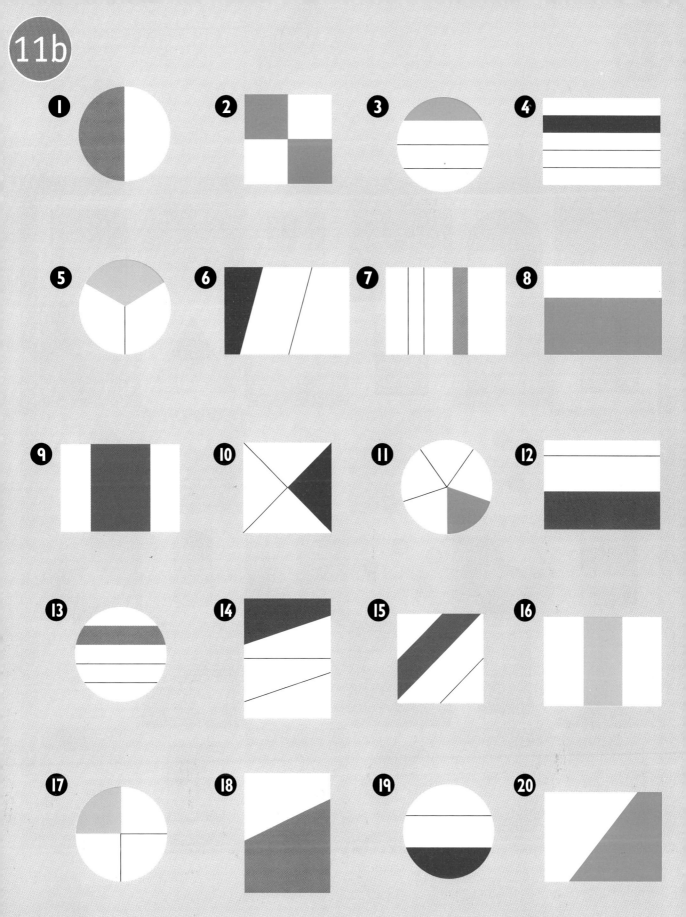

12a · How long does it take to do these things?

drink a glass of water

go three stops on a bus

watch a film at the cinema

be at school for a day

- 1 second
- 5 seconds
- 3 minutes
- 5 minutes
- 15 minutes
- 20 minutes
- 30 minutes
- 1 hour
- 2 hours
- 3 hours
- 5 hours
- 7 hours

cough

have morning playtime

eat a meal

12b **What can you do in 5 minutes?**

What can you do in 10 minutes?

eat an apple

bounce a ball

listen to a pop song

have a shower

read 2 pages of a book

write a letter

What can you do in 20 minutes?

What can you do in 1 hour? Make it up with 5, 10 and 20 minute activities.

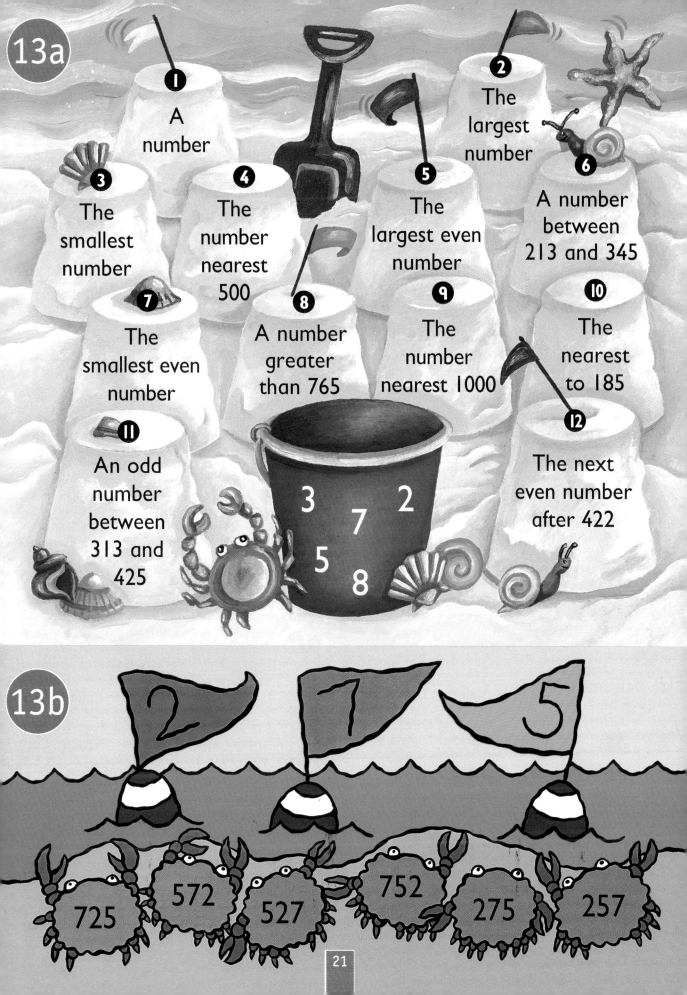

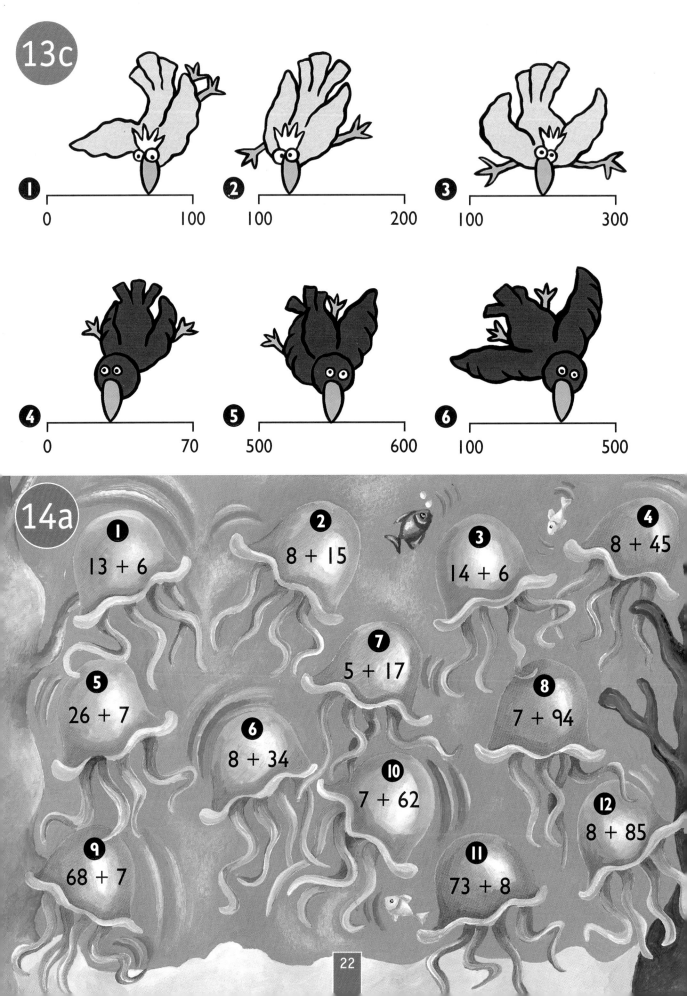

13c

1. 0 — 100
2. 100 — 200
3. 100 — 300
4. 0 — 70
5. 500 — 600
6. 100 — 500

14a

1. 13 + 6
2. 8 + 15
3. 14 + 6
4. 8 + 45
5. 26 + 7
6. 8 + 34
7. 5 + 17
8. 7 + 94
9. 68 + 7
10. 7 + 62
11. 73 + 8
12. 8 + 85

22

14b

1

+4   +4

16   20   24

$24 - 16 = 8$

2

38   40   43

$43 - 38 = \boxed{}$

3

47   55

$55 - 47 = \boxed{}$

4

168   172

$172 - 168 = \boxed{}$

5

18   20   25

$25 - 18 = \boxed{}$

6

27   30   33

$33 - 27 = \boxed{}$

7

79   84

$84 - 79 = \boxed{}$

8

477   483

$483 - 477 = \boxed{}$

14c

1 $135 + 4$

2 $485 + 3$

3 $127 + 5$

4 $236 + 7$

5 $672 - 7$

6 $405 - 396$

7 $504 - 498$

8 $324 + 6$

9 $835 + 8$

10 $302 - 298$

11 $618 + 7$

12 $703 - 697$

15

carrots
50p
per kilogram

MELONS
75p
each

STRAWBERRIES
£1.25
per punnet

75p
per kilogram

POTATOES

List A

1 How much would 2 kilograms of onions cost?

2 Jane has 90p. She buys a melon. How much does she have left?

3 Sam buys 2 grapefruit. How much does he have to pay?

4 Jo buys 1 kilogram of onions and 1 kilogram of tomatoes. How much do these cost altogether?

5 Ming buys 4 oranges. How much does she have to pay?

ONIONS
60p
per kilogram

TOMATOES
£1.20
per kg

Grapefruit
35p
each

oranges
30p
each

List B

1 How much would 2 kilograms of carrots and 2 grapefruit cost?

2 Louise has £1. She buys 1 grapefruit and 2 oranges. How much change should she get?

3 Bill buys 2 kilograms of onions and half a kilogram of tomatoes. How much does this cost?

4 Meg buys 1 kilogram of potatoes and 1 kilogram of tomatoes. She has £2. How much change should she get?

5 Sandy has £2. Does she have enough to buy 4 oranges and 3 grapefruit?

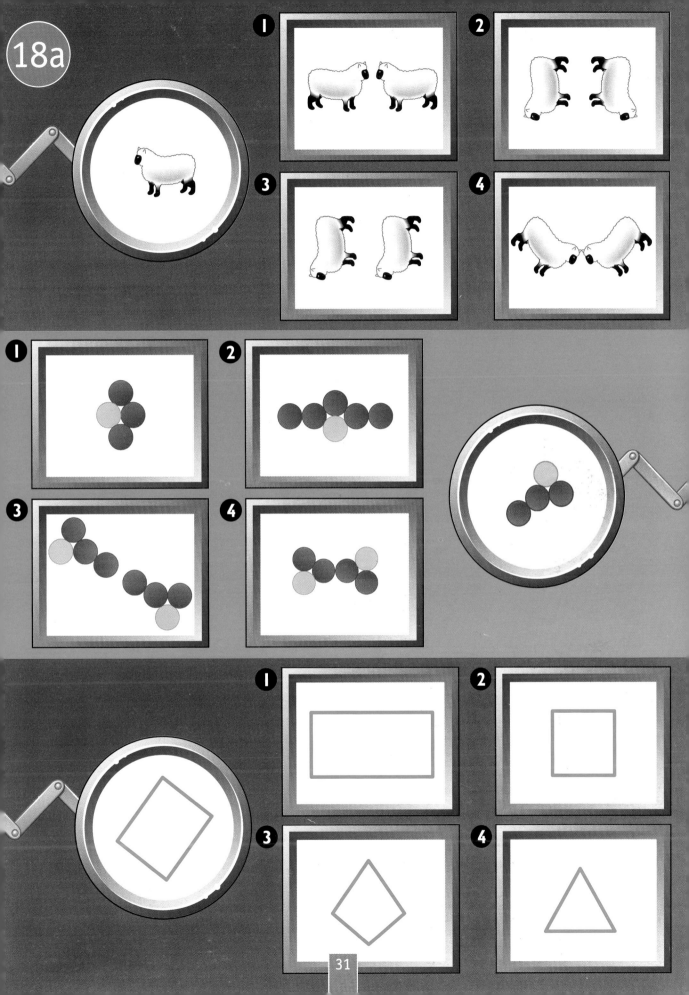

① Sanjit has collected 42 stickers. His brother gives him another 23. How many does he have now?

❷ Cleo has 30 stickers. She buys 2 more packets. Each packet has 6 stickers in it. How many stickers does she have now?

③ Anna has 23 stickers. Krysia has 24 stickers. How many do they have together?

❹ Josh had 54 stickers. He swapped 24 of them for a model car. How many stickers does he have now?

❺ Mark has 45 stickers. Harry has 32 stickers. How many more does Harry need to have the same as Mark?

19b

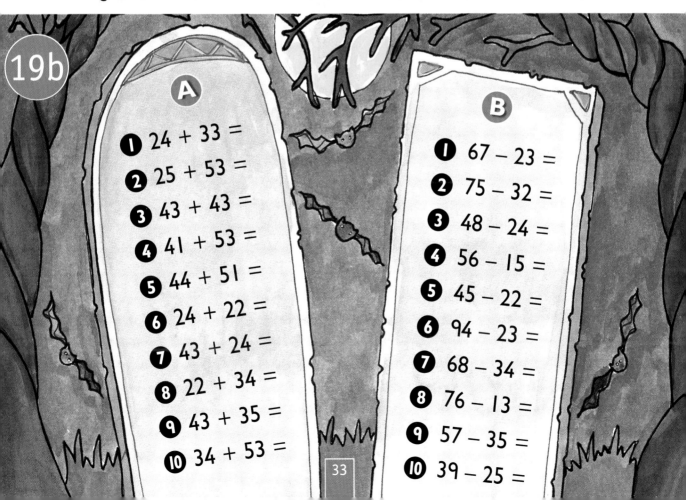

A

❶ 24 + 33 =
❷ 25 + 53 =
❸ 43 + 43 =
❹ 41 + 53 =
❺ 44 + 51 =
❻ 24 + 22 =
❼ 43 + 24 =
❽ 22 + 34 =
❾ 43 + 35 =
❿ 34 + 53 =

B

❶ 67 – 23 =
❷ 75 – 32 =
❸ 48 – 24 =
❹ 56 – 15 =
❺ 45 – 22 =
❻ 94 – 23 =
❼ 68 – 34 =
❽ 76 – 13 =
❾ 57 – 35 =
❿ 39 – 25 =

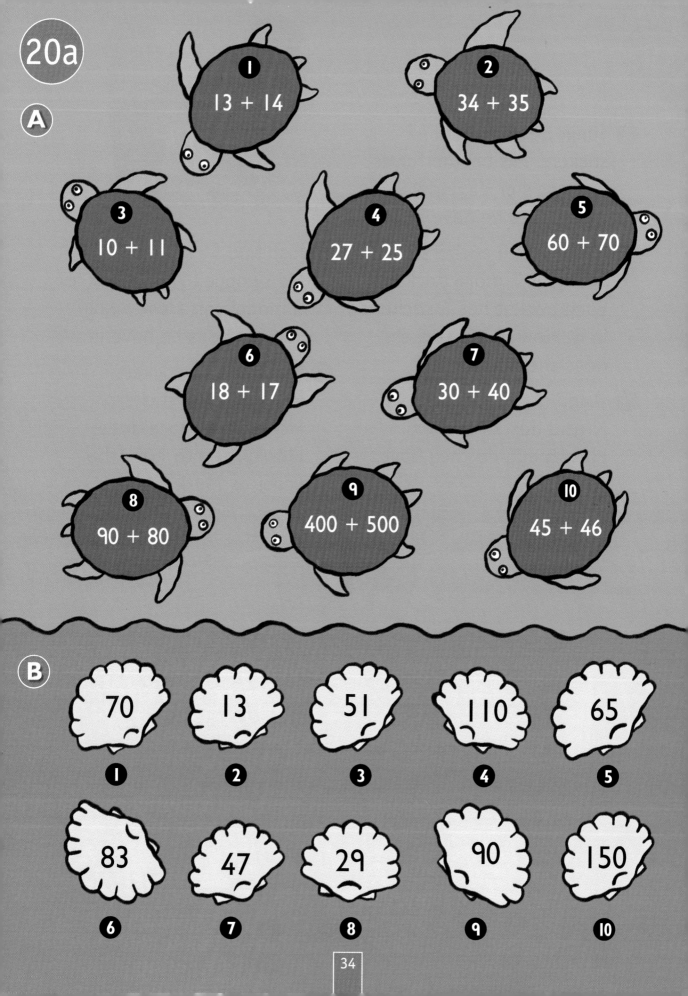

A

1. 13 + 14
2. 34 + 35
3. 10 + 11
4. 27 + 25
5. 60 + 70
6. 18 + 17
7. 30 + 40
8. 90 + 80
9. 400 + 500
10. 45 + 46

B

1. 70
2. 13
3. 51
4. 110
5. 65
6. 83
7. 47
8. 29
9. 90
10. 150

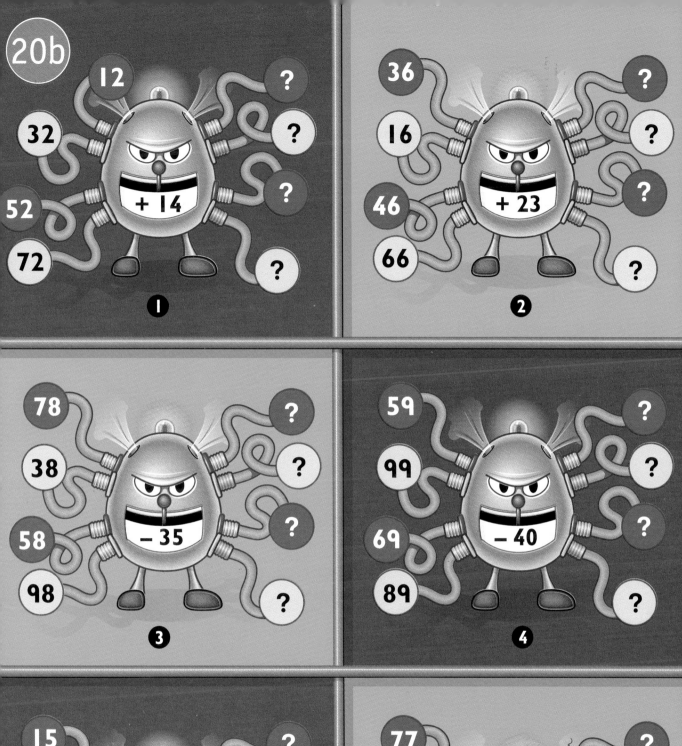

1 + 14

12 → ?
32 → ?
52 → ?
72 → ?

2 + 23

36 → ?
16 → ?
46 → ?
66 → ?

3 − 35

78 → ?
38 → ?
58 → ?
98 → ?

4 − 40

59 → ?
99 → ?
69 → ?
89 → ?

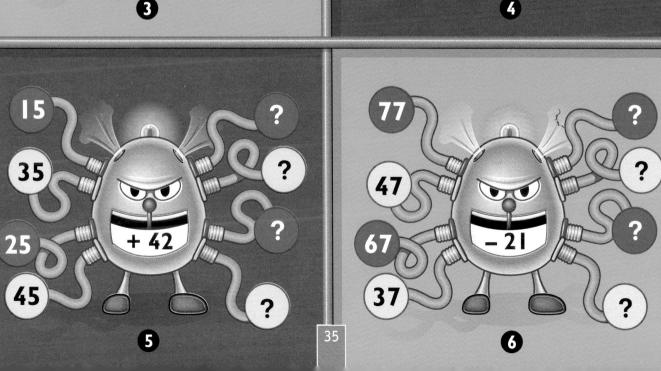

5 + 42

15 → ?
35 → ?
25 → ?
45 → ?

6 − 21

77 → ?
47 → ?
67 → ?
37 → ?

A

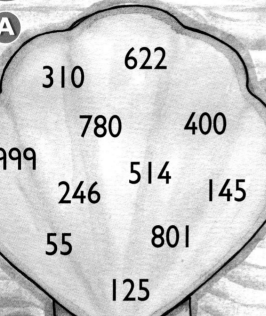

310 622
780 400
999
514
246 145
55 801
125

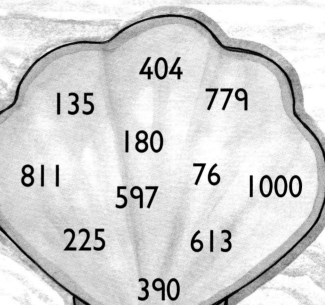

404
135 779
180
811 76 1000
597
225 613
390

B

❶ ? is less than 30

❷ ? is less than 40

❹ 465 is less than ?

❸ ? is greater than 235

❺ 700 is greater than ?

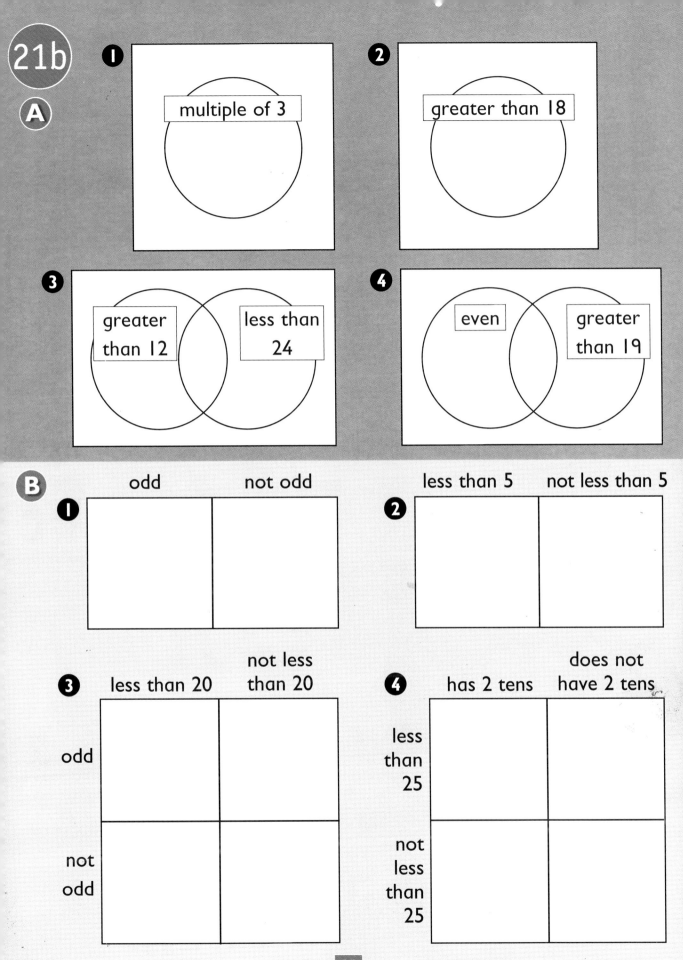

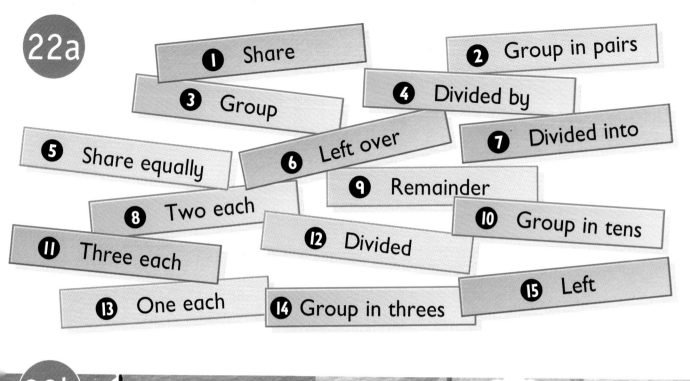

1 Share

2 Group in pairs

3 Group

4 Divided by

5 Share equally

6 Left over

7 Divided into

8 Two each

9 Remainder

10 Group in tens

11 Three each

12 Divided

13 One each

14 Group in threes

15 Left

22b

Apples

OPEN

Fresh Eggs

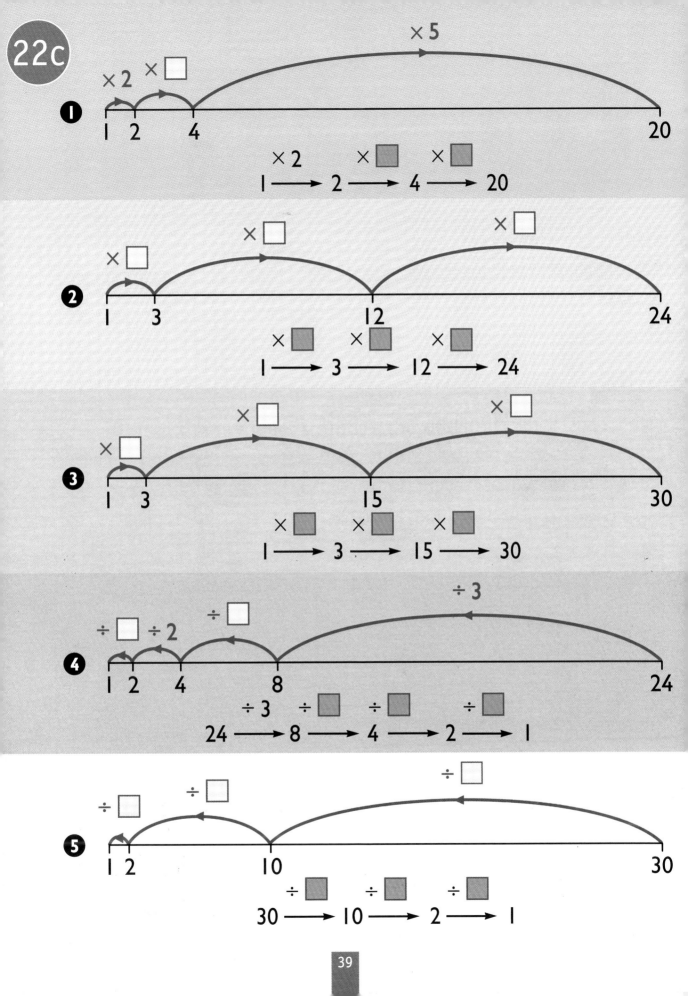

22c

1.

×2 ×□ ×5

1 2 4 20

×2 ×□ ×□
1 ⟶ 2 ⟶ 4 ⟶ 20

2.

×□ ×□ ×□

1 3 12 24

×□ ×□ ×□
1 ⟶ 3 ⟶ 12 ⟶ 24

3.

×□ ×□ ×□

1 3 15 30

×□ ×□ ×□
1 ⟶ 3 ⟶ 15 ⟶ 30

4.

÷□ ÷2 ÷□ ÷3

1 2 4 8 24

÷3 ÷□ ÷□ ÷□
24 ⟶ 8 ⟶ 4 ⟶ 2 ⟶ 1

5.

÷□ ÷□ ÷□

1 2 10 30

÷□ ÷□ ÷□
30 ⟶ 10 ⟶ 2 ⟶ 1

23 Copy and complete the number lines.

① $\frac{1}{2}$ $1\frac{1}{2}$ 2   3   5

② 12 $13\frac{1}{2}$ 16

③ 0 $\frac{3}{4}$ $1\frac{1}{4}$ $1\frac{1}{2}$ 2

④ $18\frac{1}{2}$ 20 $22\frac{1}{2}$

⑤ $2\frac{3}{4}$ $3\frac{1}{4}$ 4

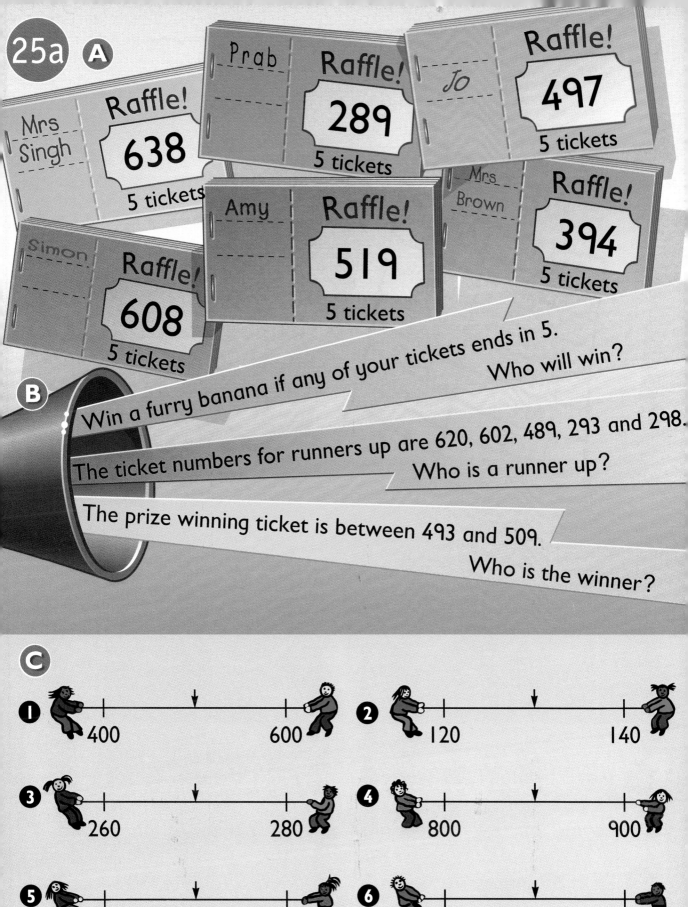

A

Mrs Singh
Raffle!
638
5 tickets

Prab
Raffle!
289
5 tickets

Jo
Raffle!
497
5 tickets

Amy
Raffle!
519
5 tickets

Mrs Brown
Raffle!
394
5 tickets

Simon
Raffle!
608
5 tickets

B

Win a furry banana if any of your tickets ends in 5. Who will win?

The ticket numbers for runners up are 620, 602, 489, 293 and 298. Who is a runner up?

The prize winning ticket is between 493 and 509. Who is the winner?

C

1   400   600

2   120   140

3   260   280

4   800   900

5   440   460

6   45   55

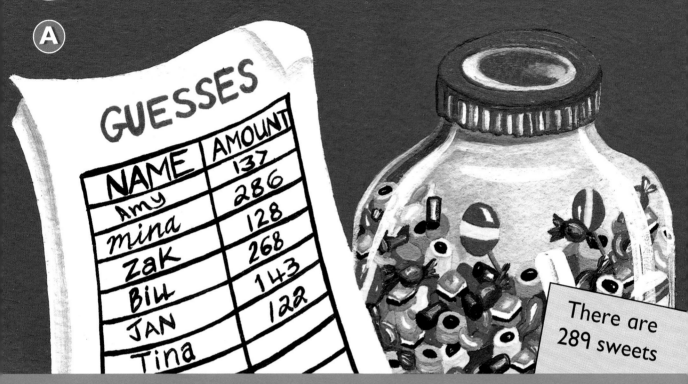

A

GUESSES

NAME	AMOUNT
Amy	137
mina	286
Zak	128
Bill	268
JAN	143
Tina	122

There are 289 sweets

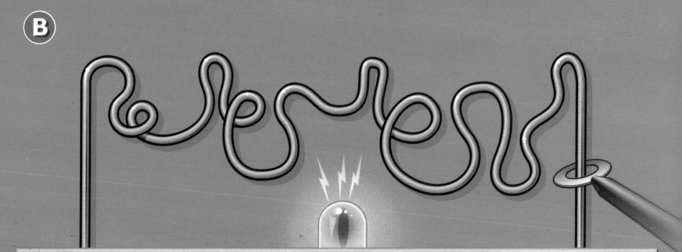

B

⬤ Amy: I minute, 30 seconds   ○ Bill: I minute, 45 seconds

○ Mina: I minute, 20 seconds   ⬤ Jan: 2 minutes, 35 seconds

⬤ Zak: 2 minutes, 40 seconds   ○ Tina: I minute, 50 seconds

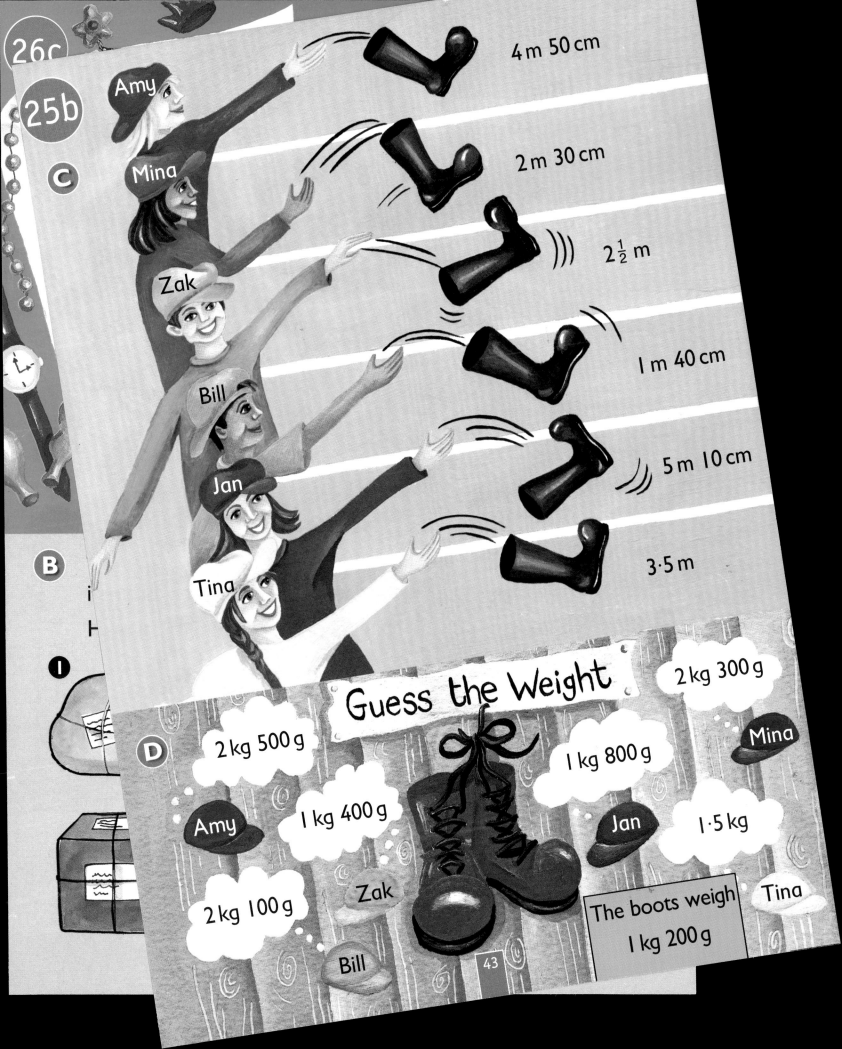

27a

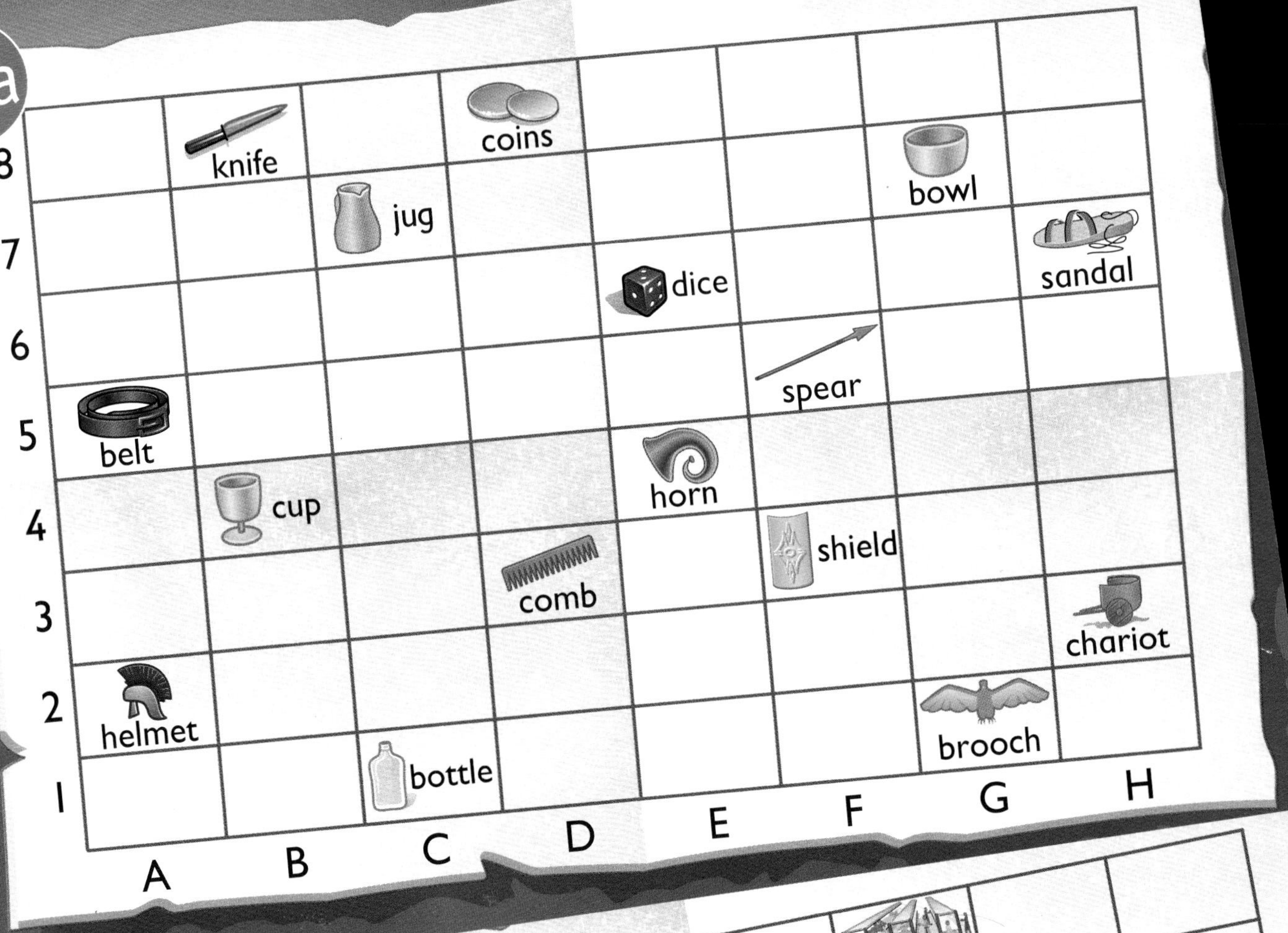
knife
coins
bowl
jug
sandal
dice
spear
belt
horn
cup
shield
comb
chariot
helmet
brooch
bottle
8
7
6
5
4
3
2
1
A
B
C
D
E
F
G
H

26b

27b

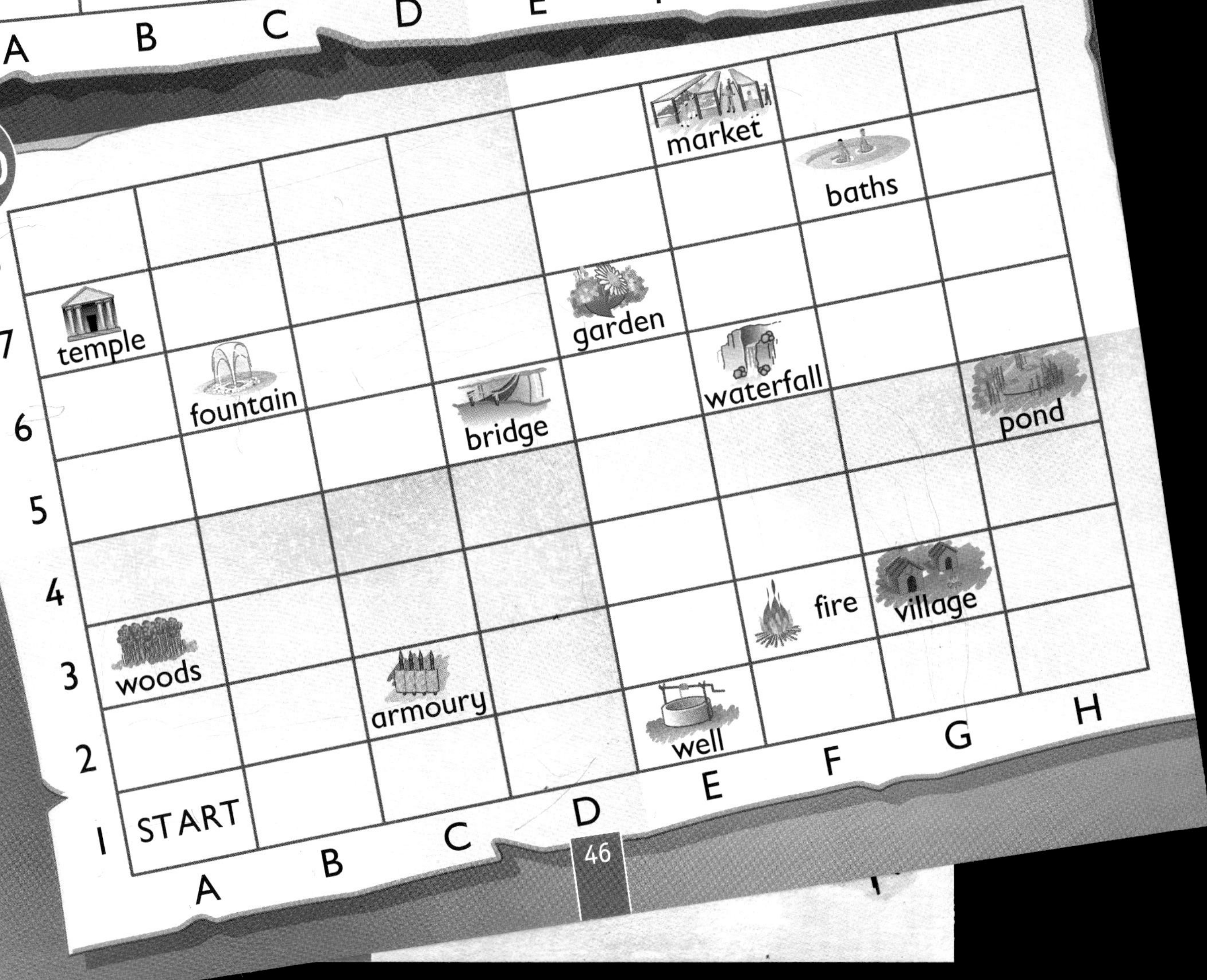
market
baths
temple
garden
fountain
waterfall
bridge
pond
fire
village
woods
armoury
well
START
8
7
6
5
4
3
2
1
A
B
C
D
E
F
G
H

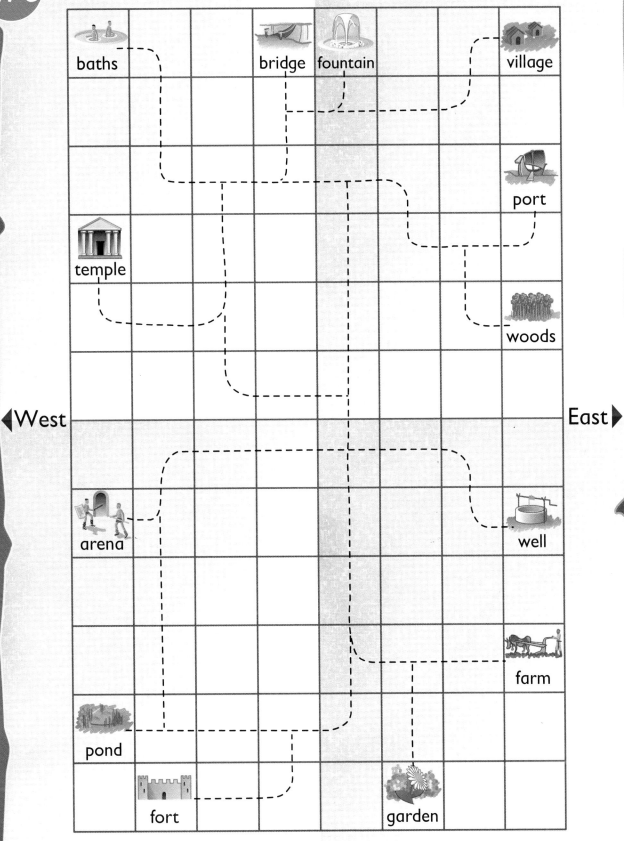

North

West

East

South

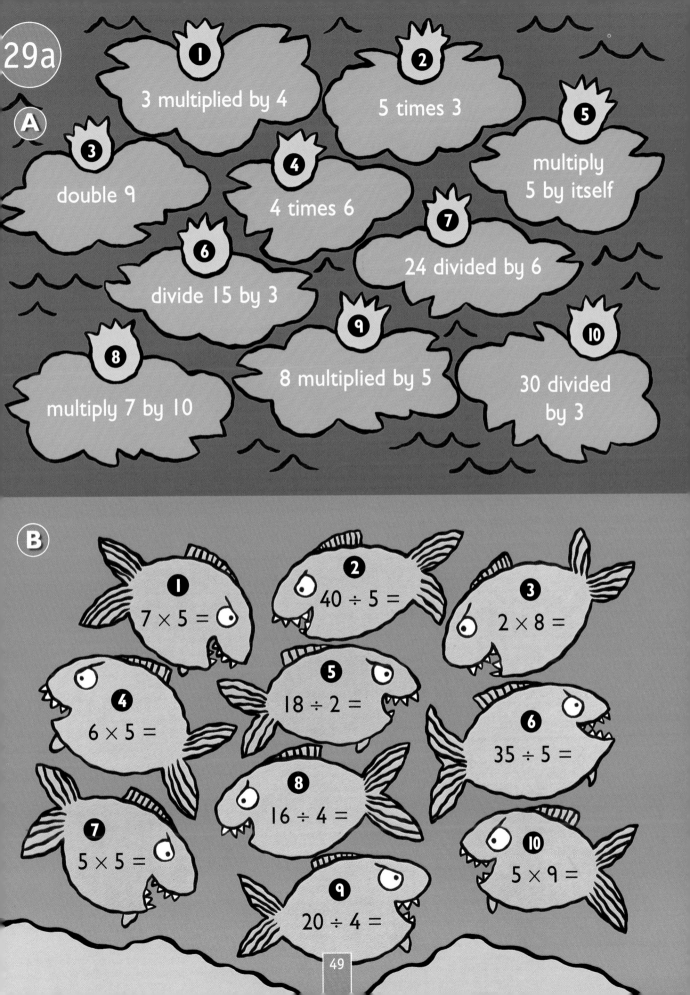

C

3

6

10

4

5

2

2

5

3

4

1

A

❶ 2 × 8 = 16   ❷ 35 ÷ 5 = 7
❸ 40 ÷ 5 = 8   ❹ 3 × 5 = 15
❺ 7 × 5 = 35   ❻ 6 × 5 = 30
❼ 20 ÷ 4 = 5   ❽ 18 ÷ 2 = 9
❾ 24 ÷ 4 = 6   ❿ 5 × 9 = 45

B

❶ Double 8

❸ $? \times 3 = 15$

❺ $30 \div 10 = ?$

❼ $5 \times ? = 50$

❾ $6 \times 4 = ?$

❷ $18 \div ? = 9$

❹ $35 \div 5 = ?$

❻ $? \times 4 = 12$

❽ $6 \div 3 = ?$

❿ $? \div 2 = 18$

29c

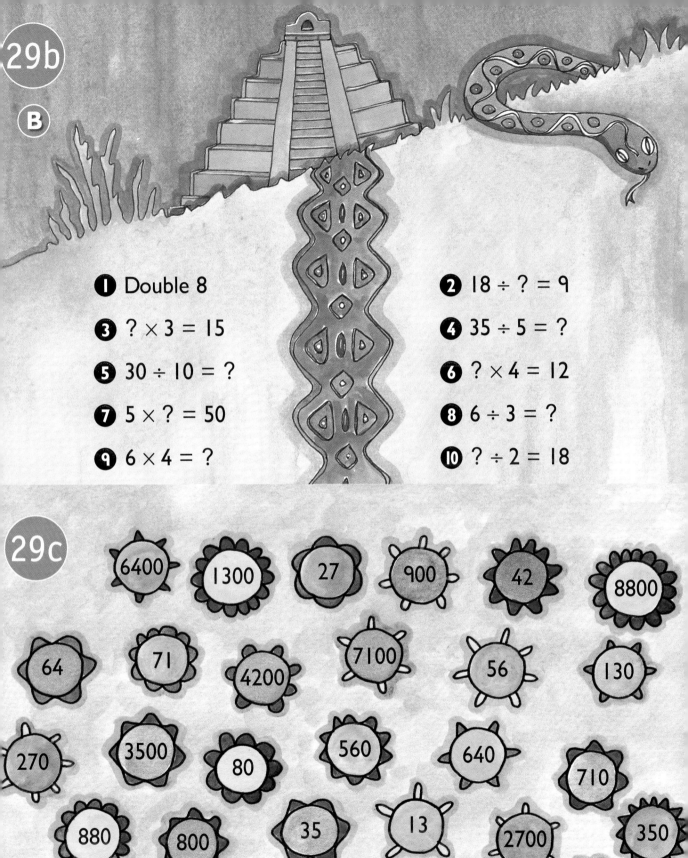

6400 1300 27 900 42 8800

64 71 4200 7100 56 130

270 3500 80 560 640 710

880 800 35 13 2700 350

88 5600 420 90 8 9000

Carroll Diagram

	Names that begin with H	Names that don't begin with H
Names with a double letter	Harriet Hannah Hassan Holly	Bobby Shanjeet Dafydd
Names without a double letter	Hugh Hugo Heidi	Parminder Tam Jasmin

Table

Children at Plumlee School with the same name

Name	Last year	This year
Amanda	3	3
Ben	9	10
Damien	1	2
Lisa	4	6
Lucy	5	3
Kamal	2	0
Sean	2	2
Yasmin	0	3

Frequency Table

Children at Peartree School with the same name

Name	Class 1	Class 2	Class 3	Class 4
Teo	1			1
Maxine		1		
Tom	1	1	3	2
Sarah	1	4	2	1
Mustafa			1	
Paul		1		1
Sharon				2

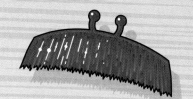

Venn Diagram

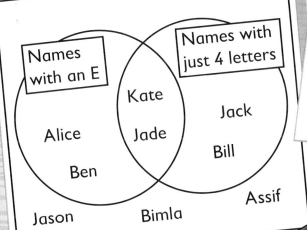

Names with an E | Names with just 4 letters

Kate
Jade
Alice
Ben
Jack
Bill
Jason
Bimla
Assif

Pictogram

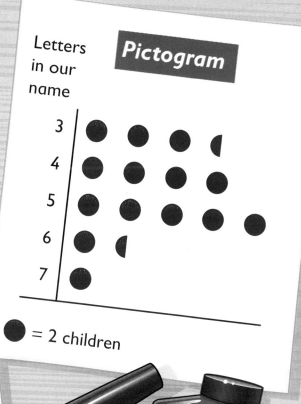

Letters in our name

3
4
5
6
7

● = 2 children

Bar Chart

Most popular names at Appleyard School

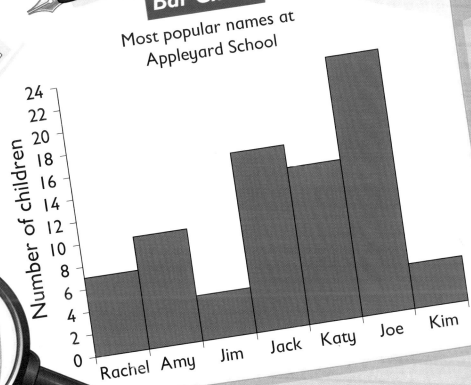

Number of children

24
22
20
18
16
14
12
10
8
6
4
2
0

Rachel Amy Jim Jack Katy Joe Kim

31a

Circle 1:
15
54 27 32
45

Circle 2:
42
35 58 13
24

31b

A

1
```
  41
+ 12
----
  50
```

2
```
  51
+ 21
----
  █0
```
3
3

3
```
  63
+ 25
----
  88
```

4
```
  72
+ 3█
----
  90

  95
```

5
```
   2█
+ 3█
----
  80

   6█

   6█
```

B

65 + 32 =

58 + 27 =

60 + 23 =

20 + 60 =

62 + 44 =

14 + 92 =

23 + 54 =

28 + 63 =

36 + 34 =

74 + 4 =

74 + 53 =

9 + 54 =

53 + 1 =

4 + 20 =

45 + 15 =

96 + 24 =

20 + 8 =

73 + 64 =

12 + 23 =

74 + 61 =

45 + 55 =

Mac Diner

Write these as number sentences.
Find the answers.

1 Sixty-seven take away thirty-five.

2 How many more than twenty-nine is fifty-two?

3 Find the difference between fifty-four and twenty-six.

4 Add together thirty-two and forty-three.

5 Subtract forty-five from ninety-two.

6 What is twenty-three more than forty-seven?

7 Take thirty-eight away from seventy-six.

8 Eighty-one subtract thirty-four.

Mac Diner

Make up four more sentences like these.

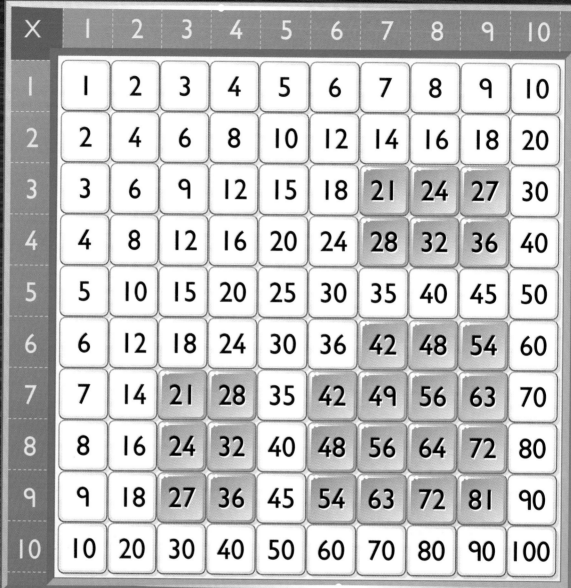

×	1	2	3	4	5	6	7	8	9	10
1	1	2	3	4	5	6	7	8	9	10
2	2	4	6	8	10	12	14	16	18	20
3	3	6	9	12	15	18	21	24	27	30
4	4	8	12	16	20	24	28	32	36	40
5	5	10	15	20	25	30	35	40	45	50
6	6	12	18	24	30	36	42	48	54	60
7	7	14	21	28	35	42	49	56	63	70
8	8	16	24	32	40	48	56	64	72	80
9	9	18	27	36	45	54	63	72	81	90
10	10	20	30	40	50	60	70	80	90	100

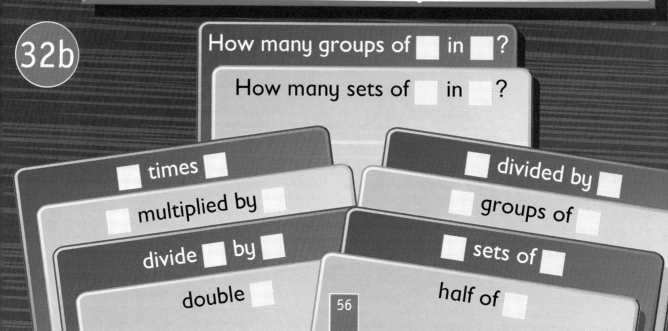

How many groups of ▢ in ▢?

How many sets of ▢ in ▢?

▢ times ▢

▢ divided by ▢

▢ multiplied by ▢

▢ groups of ▢

divide ▢ by ▢

▢ sets of ▢

double ▢

half of ▢

Joke Shop

1 There are 32 children. How many packets must I buy so everyone has a plastic spider?

2 I have 46p. How many packets of pepper sweets can I buy?

3 There are 43 children. How many Icy Fly trays must I buy so that everyone can have one fly in an ice cube?

Joke Shop

4 How many packets of itching powder can I buy for £1.75?

5 Packing boxes hold 10 plastic biscuits. How many boxes must the shopkeeper use to pack all the biscuits?

6 I have 94p. How many 'nails through the finger' can I buy?

33a

olive oil · Cola · Vinegar · Lemonade · SOY SAUCE · Orange · GINGER ALE · Vanilla Essence · BROWN SAUCE · Bitter Lemon

33b

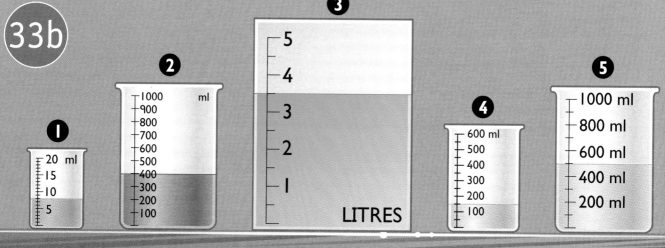

1 — 20 ml, 15, 10, 5

2 — 1000 ml, 900, 800, 700, 600, 500, 400, 300, 200, 100

3 — 5, 4, 3, 2, 1 LITRES

4 — 600 ml, 500, 400, 300, 200, 100

5 — 1000 ml, 800 ml, 600 ml, 400 ml, 200 ml

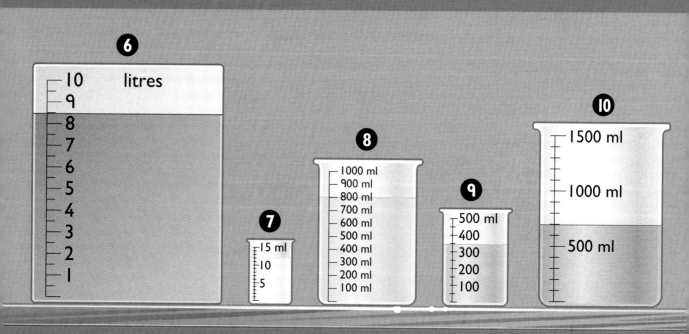

6 — 10 litres, 9, 8, 7, 6, 5, 4, 3, 2, 1

7 — 15 ml, 10, 5

8 — 1000 ml, 900 ml, 800 ml, 700 ml, 600 ml, 500 ml, 400 ml, 300 ml, 200 ml, 100 ml

9 — 500 ml, 400, 300, 200, 100

10 — 1500 ml, 1000 ml, 500 ml

THE WACKY TOY C⁰

A ring watch £1.50

Furry spider 60p

See-through plastic wallet 75p

Key ring torch £1.25

BARGAIN 2 spiders for £1.00

Smallest kite in the world £2.05

floating paper **FLOWERS** 5p

NEW

Nuts and bolts necklace 90p

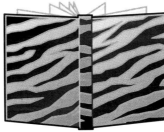

Tiger fur notebook £1.05

MUSICAL SOCKS £2.25

10p **CURLING FISH**

35p

Wind-up mouse

mini jigsaw puzzle £1.15

Windscreen wiper sunglasses £2.00

1 If everyone in your group lay head-to-toe on the ground, how long a line would you make?

What if everyone in the class lay down head-to-toe?

2 How many teeth are there between all the children in your group?

How many teeth altogether in the class?

3 If everyone in your group held hands in a long line with arms stretched out, how long would the line be?

How long a line would the whole class make?

What's my number?

1
I'm thinking of a number. I add 4 to it. I double the answer. I get 16.

2
Start with 4, double it, add 3. What's your answer?

3
I'm thinking of a number. I add 8 to it. I halve the answer. I get 10.

4
I'm thinking of a number. I multiply it by 4. I add 5. I get 29.

5
I'm thinking of a number. I divide it by 5. I subtract 4. I get 2.

6
I'm thinking of a number. I divide it by 3. I add 13. I get 19.

7
I'm thinking of a number. I subtract 3 from it. I multiply by 2. I get 2.

8
I'm thinking of a number. I multiply it by 8. I subtract 6. I get 18.

9
Start with 5 add 6, double this number. What's your answer?

10
I'm thinking of a number. I add 9 to it. I divide it by 2. I get 10.

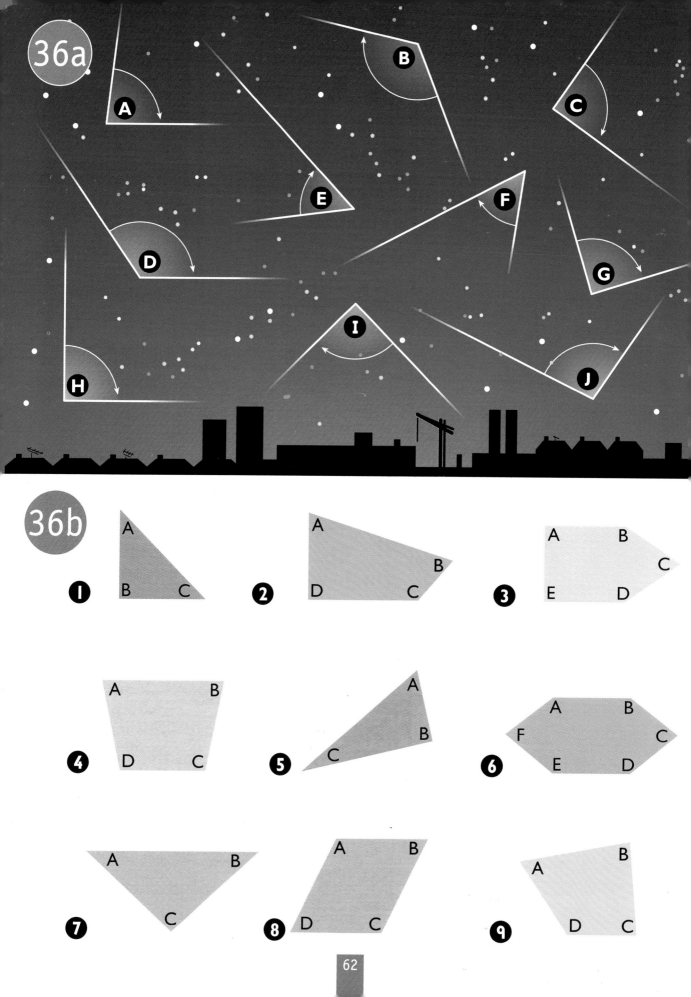